BOOK TWO

30 note spelling lessons

By David Carr Glover

David Carr Glover
PIANO LIBRARY

FOREWORD

These 30 NOTE SPELLING LESSONS are for the reinforcement of the music fundamentals found in Level One and Level Two of the David Carr Glover Piano Library. They present note spelling on the grand staff, leger lines and spaces, chord note spelling, whole steps and half steps, forming tetrachords and major scales and notes and rests in $\frac{4}{4}$, $\frac{3}{4}$, $\frac{2}{4}$, and $\frac{6}{8}$ Meter.

For further reinforcement of music fundamentals at this level of study the following music games published by Belwin-Mills Publishing Corp. and created by Helen Wunnenberg and David Carr Glover are recommended. They are: Music Forte (Music Bingo), Music Match - Go, and Music Cross - Go.

CONTENTS

Lesson	Page
1. Note Spelling — Bass Staff Lines	3
2. Note Spelling — Bass Staff Spaces	4
3. Note Spelling — Treble Staff Lines	5
4. Note Spelling — Treble Staff Spaces	6
5. Note Spelling — Grand Staff	7
6. Note Spelling — Inner Leger Lines and Spaces	8
7. Note Spelling — Outer Leger Lines and Spaces	9
8. Note Spelling — Accidentals	10
9. Half Steps and Whole Steps	11
10. Forming Tetrachords	12
11. Forming Major Scales	13
12. Note Spelling in Specific Keys	14
13. Enharmonic Notes	15
14. Matching Notes and Rests	16
15. Note Spelling — Intervals	17
16. Note Spelling — The I Chord	18
17. Note Spelling — The V7 Chord	19
18. Note Spelling — The IV Chord	20
19. Notes and Rests Used in $\frac{4}{4}$, $\frac{3}{4}$, and $\frac{2}{4}$ Meter	21
20. Note Spelling and Beat Counts	22
21. Note Spelling — Grand Staff	23
22. Notes and Rests Used in $\frac{6}{8}$ Meter	24
23. Note Spelling and Beat Counts	25
24. Note Spelling and Measure Bars	26
25. Drawing Notes — Grand Staff	27
26. Drawing and Spelling Accidentals	28
27. Note Spelling in Specific Keys	29
28. Note Spelling — Primary Chords	30
29. Note Spelling — Intervals	31
30. Note Spelling — Grand Staff	32

1977 BELWIN-MILLS PUBLISHING CORP.
All Rights Administered by WARNER BROS. PUBLICATIONS U.S. INC.
All Rights Reserved

LESSON No. 1 - Note Spelling - Bass Staff Lines

Write letter names for the following Bass Staff Line Notes.

Row 1: A B F D G B F D A F G B

Row 2: G A B F D B F D A F G A

Row 3: F A D G B F D A B G B F

Row 4: B G F A D G F B D A B G

Draw notes as directed for the following letter names on the Bass Staff Lines.

Use Whole Notes.

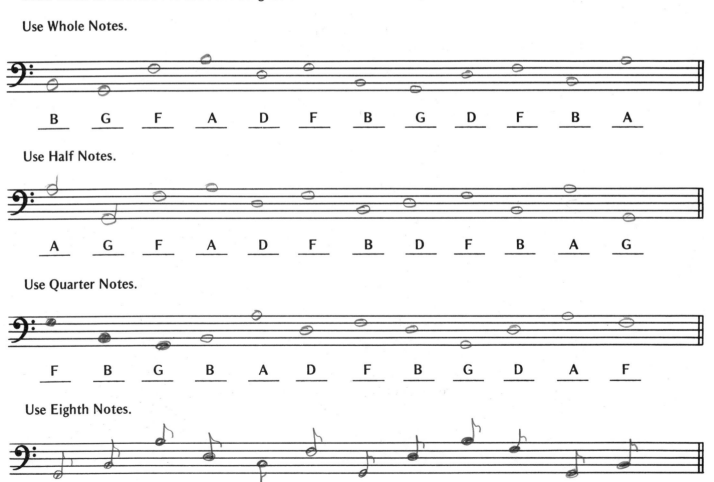

B G F A D F B G D F B A

Use Half Notes.

A G F A D F B D F B A G

Use Quarter Notes.

F B G B A D F B G D A F

Use Eighth Notes.

G B A D B F G D A F G B

LESSON No. 2 - Note Spelling - Bass Staff Spaces

Write letter names for the following Bass Staff Space Notes.

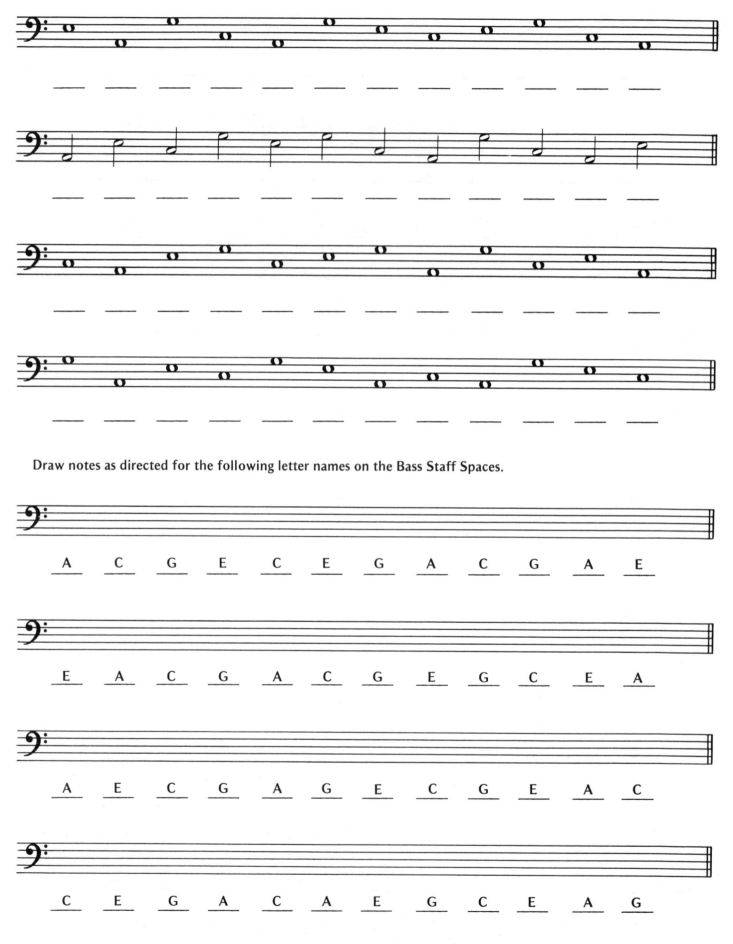

Draw notes as directed for the following letter names on the Bass Staff Spaces.

A C G E C E G A C G A E

E A C G A C G E G C E A

A E C G A G E C G E A C

C E G A C A E G C E A G

LESSON No. 3 - Note Spelling - Treble Staff Lines

Write letter names for the following Treble Staff Line Notes.

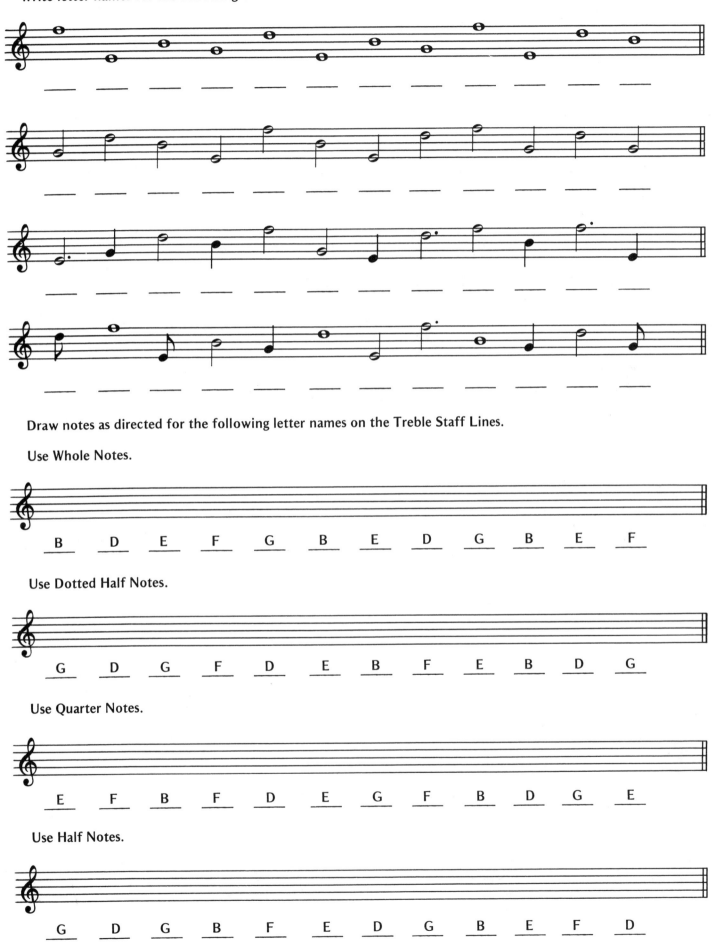

Draw notes as directed for the following letter names on the Treble Staff Lines.

Use Whole Notes.

B   D   E   F   G   B   E   D   G   B   E   F

Use Dotted Half Notes.

G   D   G   F   D   E   B   F   E   B   D   G

Use Quarter Notes.

E   F   B   F   D   E   G   F   B   D   G   E

Use Half Notes.

G   D   G   B   F   E   D   G   B   E   F   D

FDL 736

LESSON No. 4 - Note Spelling - Treble Staff Spaces

Write letter names for the following Treble Staff Space Notes.

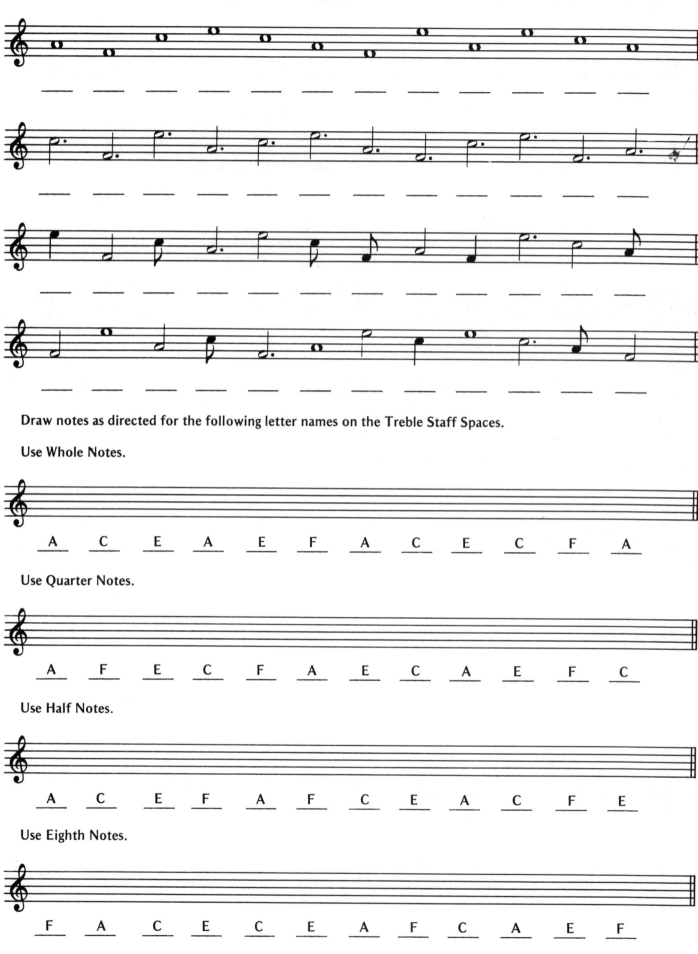

Draw notes as directed for the following letter names on the Treble Staff Spaces.

Use Whole Notes.

A C E A E F A C E C F A

Use Quarter Notes.

A F E C F A E C A E F C

Use Half Notes.

A C E F A F C E A C F E

Use Eighth Notes.

F A C E C E A F C A E F

LESSON No. 5 - Note Spelling - Grand Staff

Write letter names for the following notes. They spell words.

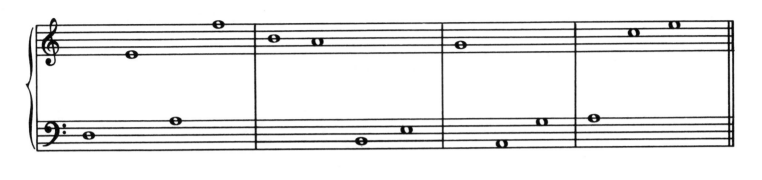

- - - - - - - - - - - - - - -

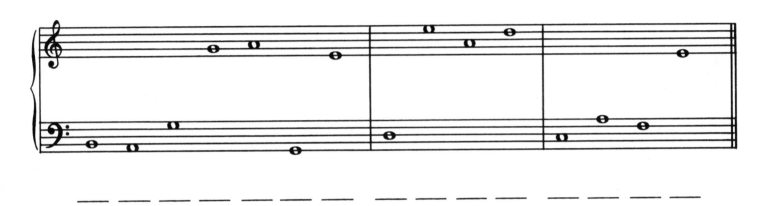

- - - - - - - - - - - - - - -

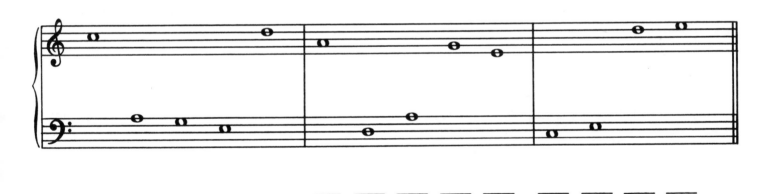

- - - - - - - - - - - - - - -

- - - - - - - - - - - - - - -

FDL 736

LESSON No. 6 - Note Spelling - Inner Leger Lines And Spaces

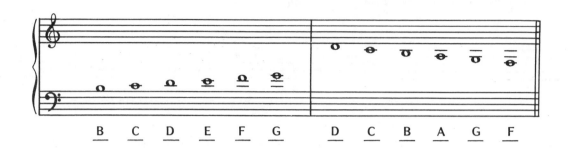

B C D E F G   D C B A G F

LESSON No. 7 - Note Spelling - Outer Leger Lines And Spaces

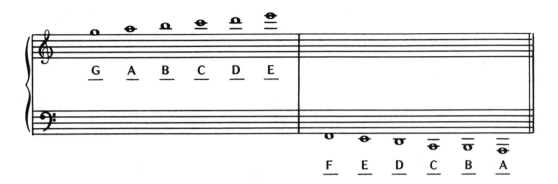

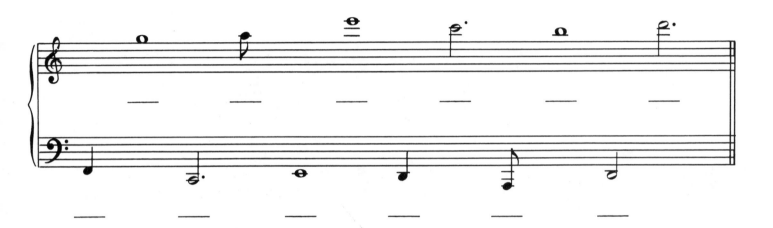

LESSON No. 8 - Note Spelling - Accidentals

When sharp, flat, and natural signs appear before notes in music they are called ACCIDENTALS.

A sharp before a note means to play the very next key UP to the right.

A flat before a note means to play the very next key DOWN to the left.

A natural before a note cancels a sharp or flat.

Write letter names and add Accidentals for the following notes.

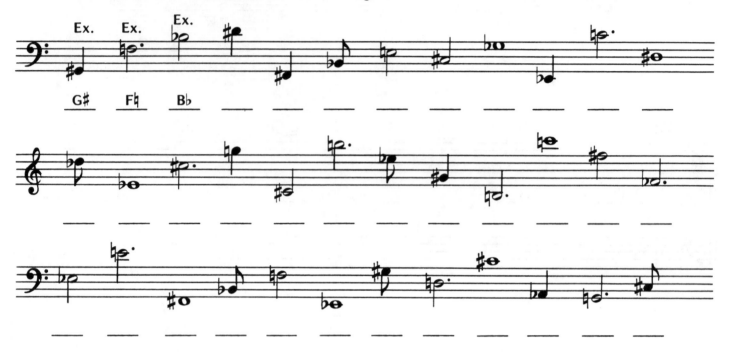

Draw notes with Accidentals before them as directed.

Use Half Notes.

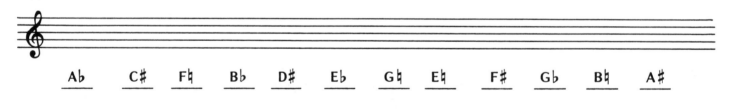

Use Whole Notes.

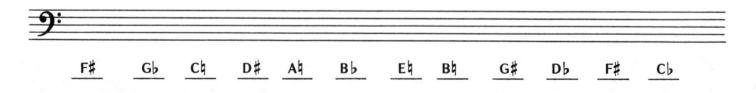

Use Quarter Notes.

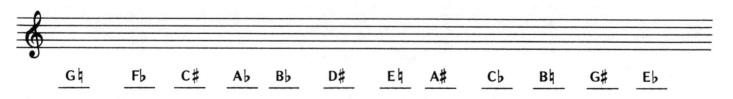

LESSON No. 9 - Half Steps And Whole Steps

A Half Step is from one key to the next key with no key in between.

A Whole Step is from one key to another key with <u>one</u> key in between.

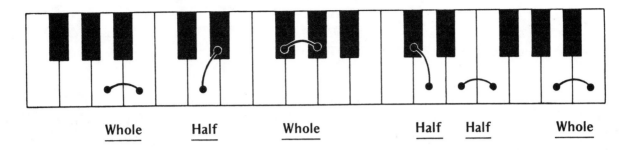

Whole   Half   Whole   Half   Half   Whole

Write H for Half Step and W for Whole Step.

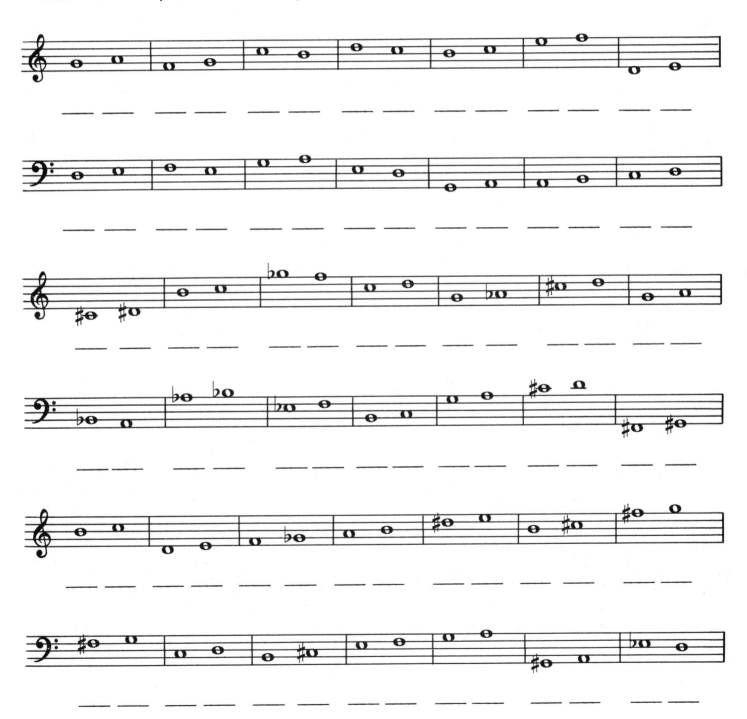

LESSON No. 10 - Forming Tetrachords

A Tetrachord is two whole steps and a half-step arranged in the following succession:

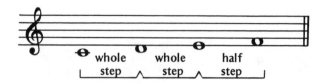

By adding sharps or flats when necessary change the following groups of notes to Tetrachords. In the brackets below the notes write W for Whole Step and H for Half-Stp. Remember they must be arranged in this succession: Whole Step — Whole Step — Half Step.

Ex.

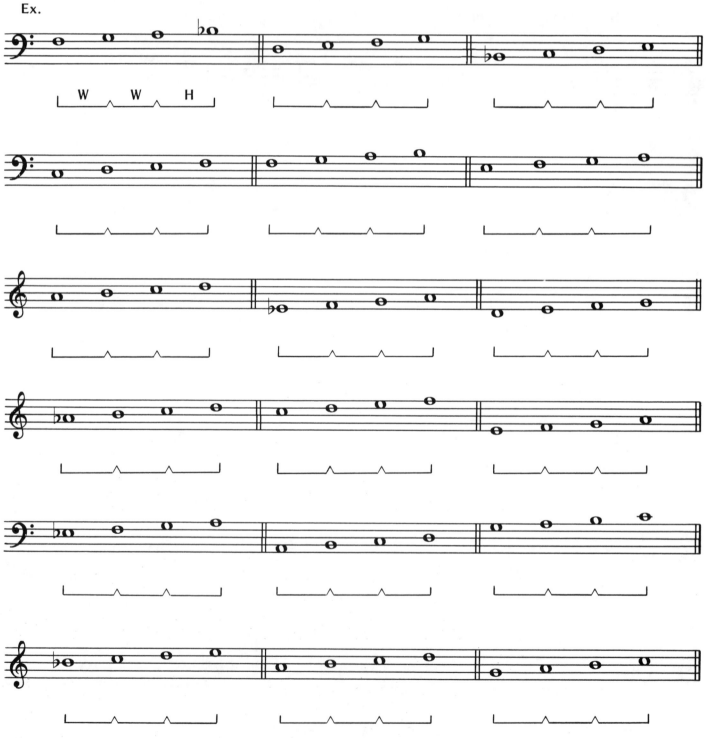

LESSON No. 11 - Forming Major Scales

Two Tetrachords diveded by a Whole Step form a Major Scale.

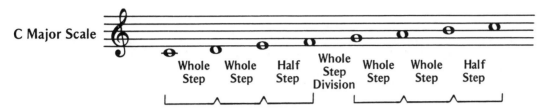

By adding sharps or flats, change the following groups of notes to Major Scales. In the brackets below the notes write W for Whole Step and H for Half Step. Remember they must be arranged in this succession: Whole Step — Whole Step — Half Step — Whole Step Division — Whole Step — Whole Step — Half Step.

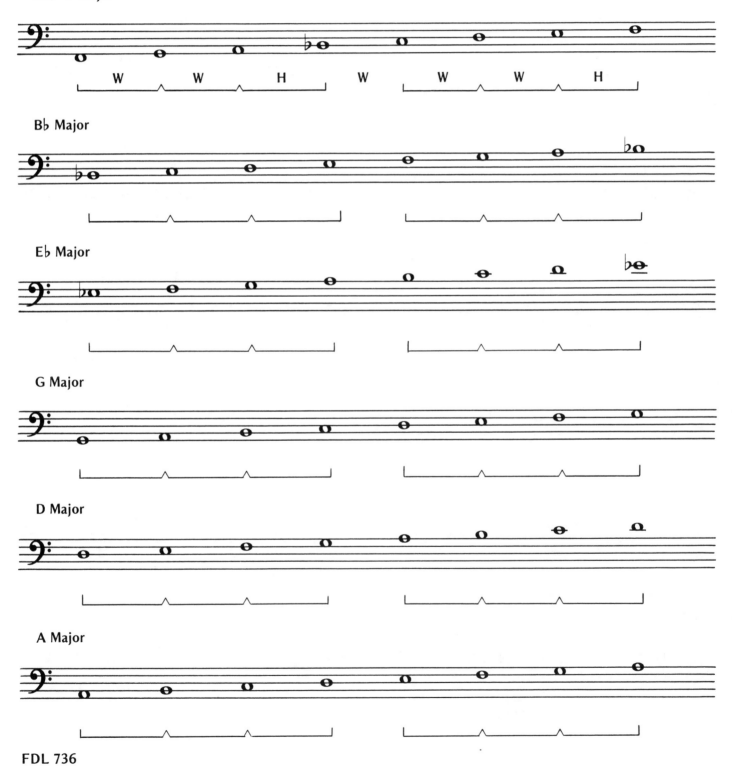

FDL 736

LESSON No. 12 - Note Spelling In Specific Keys

Write letter names for the following notes. Be sure to observe the Key Signature.

LESSON No. 13 - Enharmonic Notes

Many notes have different letter names but are played on the same key. Ex. - G♯ and A♭. These are called ENHARMONIC NOTES.

On the Staffs below draw a note that is different from the given note but would be played on the same key.

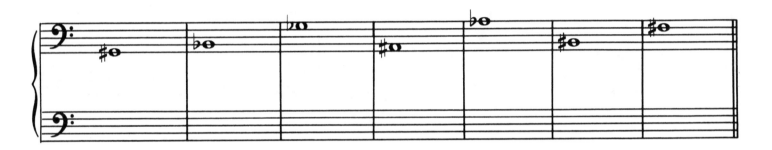

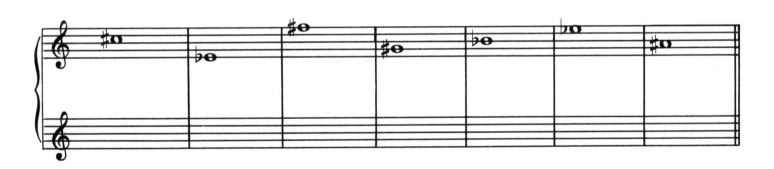

FDL 736

LESSON No. 14 - Matching Notes And Rests

Draw a note that matches the given rest.

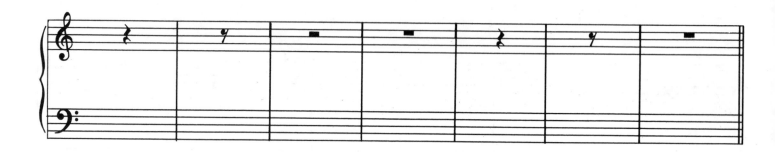

Draw a rest that matches the given note.

LESSON No. 15 - Note Spelling - Intervals

Write letter names for the following notes of the given Intervals.

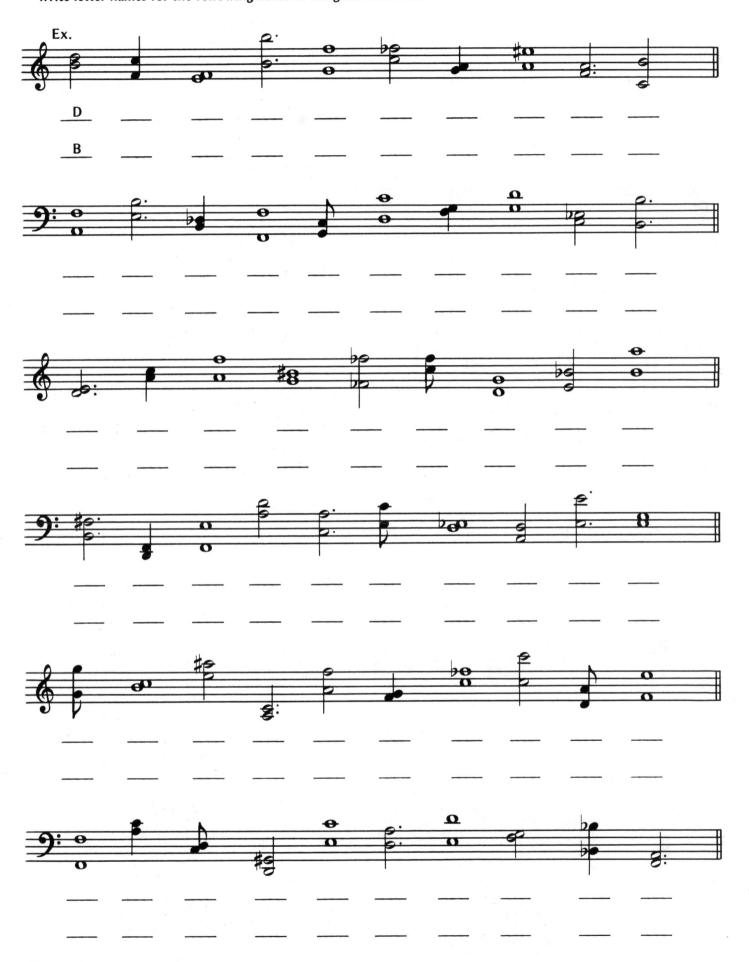

LESSON No. 16 - Note Spelling - The I Chord

Write letter names for the notes in each chord.

LESSON No. 17 - Note Spelling - The V7 Chord

Write letter names for the notes in each chord.

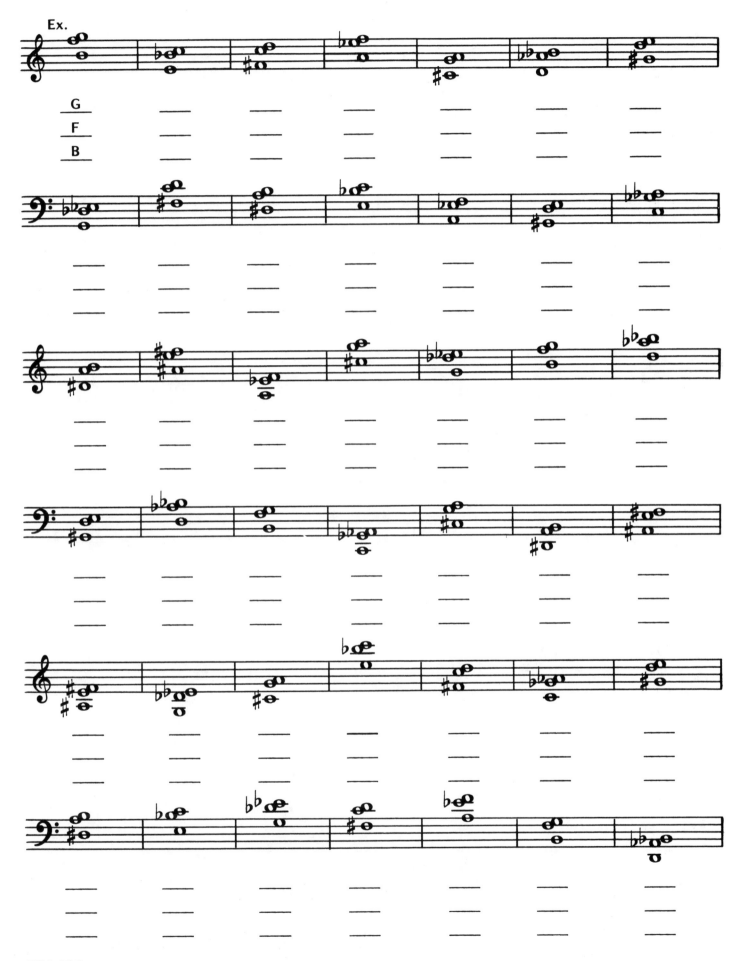

FDL 736

LESSON No. 18 - Note Spelling - The IV Chord

Write letter names for the notes in each chord.

LESSON No. 19 - Notes And Rests Used In $\frac{4}{4}$, $\frac{3}{4}$, And $\frac{2}{4}$ Meter

Table

NOTES	RESTS	NAMES	BEAT COUNTS
o	▬	WHOLE	4
𝅗𝅥.	(▬ 𝄽) or (▬·)	DOTTED HALF	3
𝅗𝅥	▬	HALF	2
♩.	(𝄽 𝄾) or (𝄽·)	DOTTED QUARTER	1½
♩	𝄽	QUARTER	1
♪	𝄾	EIGHTH	½

Write the number of Beat Counts for each of the following notes and rests when used in $\frac{4}{4}$, $\frac{3}{4}$, and $\frac{2}{4}$ Meter.

_____ _____ _____ _____ _____ _____ _____ _____ _____ _____ _____ _____

Change the following Whole Notes to notes that match the given Beat Counts when used in $\frac{4}{4}$, $\frac{3}{4}$, and $\frac{2}{4}$ Meter.

3   2   1½   1   ½   4   2   1

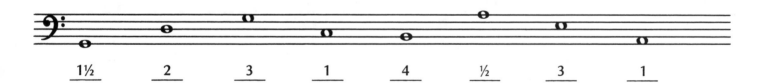

1½   2   3   1   4   ½   3   1

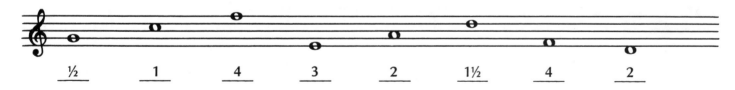

½   1   4   3   2   1½   4   2

Draw Rests that match the given Beat Counts when used in $\frac{4}{4}$, $\frac{3}{4}$, and $\frac{2}{4}$ Meter.

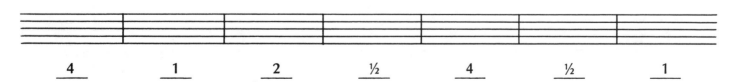

4   1   2   ½   4   ½   1

FDL 736

LESSON No. 20 - Note Spelling And Beat Counts

Write letter names and the Beat Counts for the following notes when used in $\frac{4}{4}$, $\frac{3}{4}$, and $\frac{2}{4}$ Meter.

Write the Beat Counts for the following rests when used in $\frac{4}{4}$, $\frac{3}{4}$, and $\frac{2}{4}$ Meter.

LESSON No. 21 - Note Spelling - Grand Staff

Write letter names for the following Grand Staff notes. They spell words.

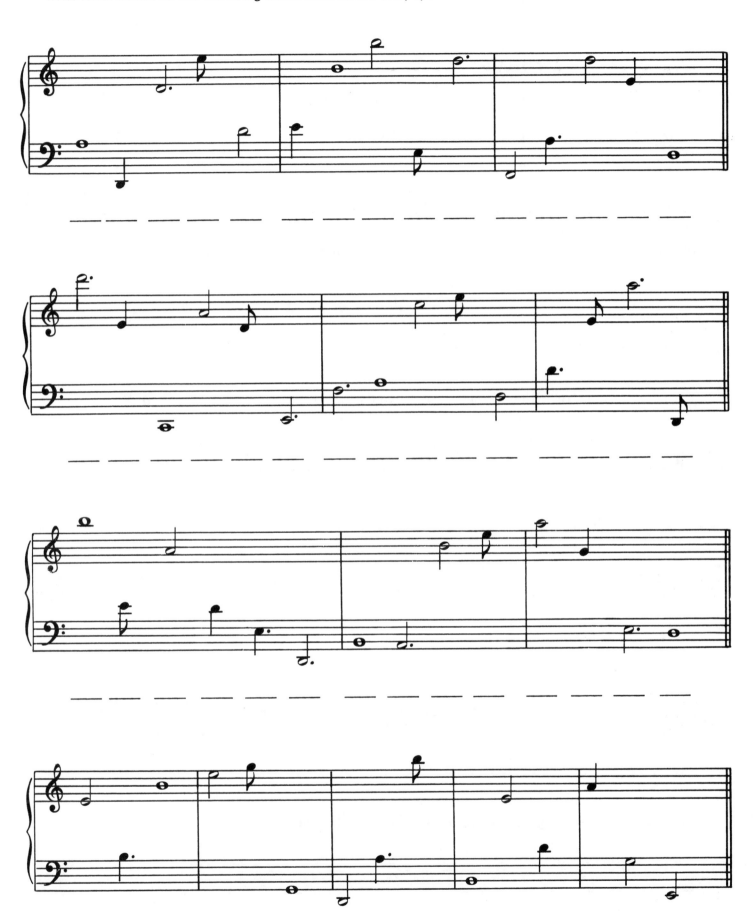

LESSON No. 22 - Notes And Rests Used In $\frac{6}{8}$ Meter

Table			
NOTES	RESTS	NAMES	BEAT COUNTS
𝅗𝅥.	(𝄽· 𝄽·) or (𝄻)	HALF	6
𝅗𝅥.	𝄽·	DOTTED HALF	3
𝅘𝅥	𝄽	QUARTER	2
𝅘𝅥𝅮	𝄾	EIGHTH	1

Write the number of Beat Counts for each of the following notes and rests when used in $\frac{4}{4}$, $\frac{3}{4}$, and $\frac{2}{4}$ Meter.

Change the following Whole Notes to notes that match the given Beat Counts when used in $\frac{6}{8}$ Meter.

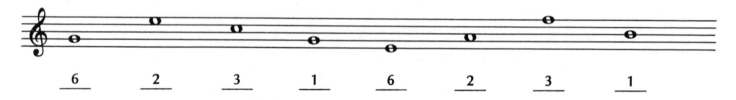

| 6 | 2 | 3 | 1 | 6 | 2 | 3 | 1 |

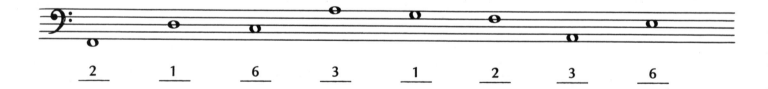

| 2 | 1 | 6 | 3 | 1 | 2 | 3 | 6 |

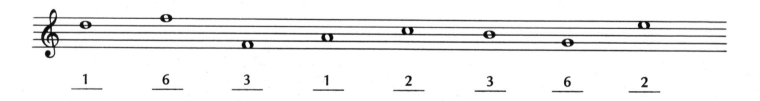

| 1 | 6 | 3 | 1 | 2 | 3 | 6 | 2 |

Draw Rests that match the given Beat Counts when used in $\frac{6}{8}$ Meter.

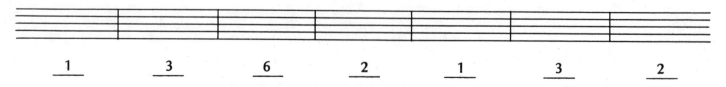

| 1 | 3 | 6 | 2 | 1 | 3 | 2 |

LESSON No. 23 - Note Spelling And Beat Counts

Write letter names and the Beat Counts for the following notes when used in **6/8** Meter.

Ex.

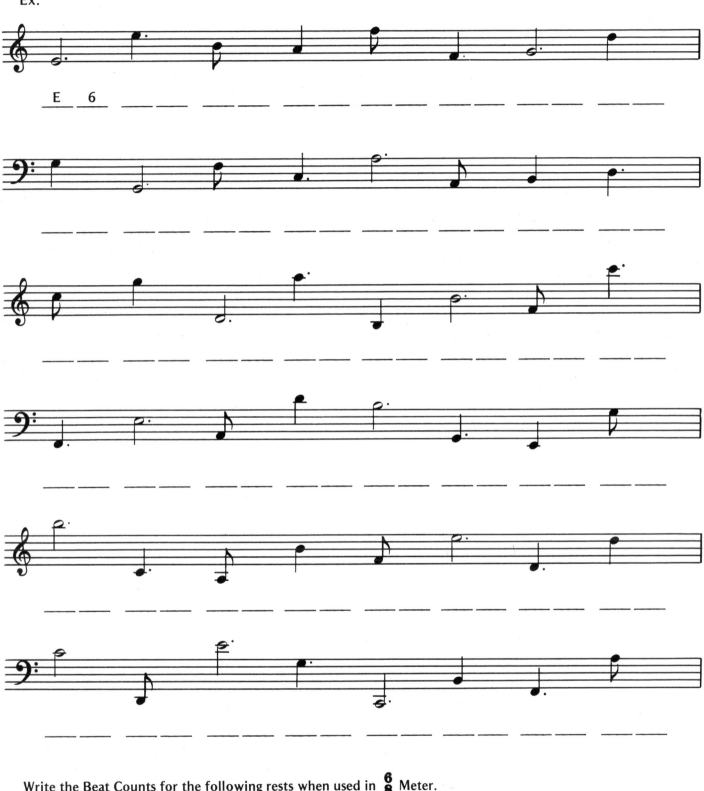

Write the Beat Counts for the following rests when used in **6/8** Meter.

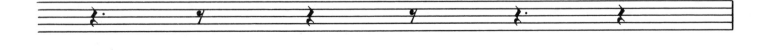

FDL 736

LESSON No. 24 - Note Spelling And Measure Bars

Add Measure Bars to the following music and write letter names for the notes.

LESSON No. 25 - Drawing Notes - Grand Staff

Draw two line notes for each given letter name. Place one on Bass Staff and one on Treble Staff. Some will be leger line notes.

Use Quarter Notes.

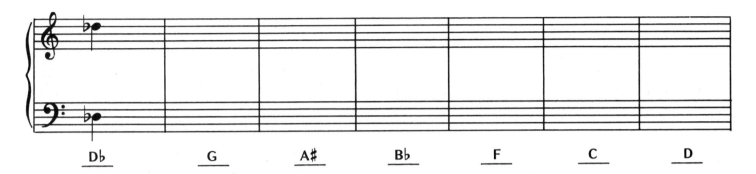

Db   G   A#   Bb   F   C   D

Continue using dotted Half Notes.

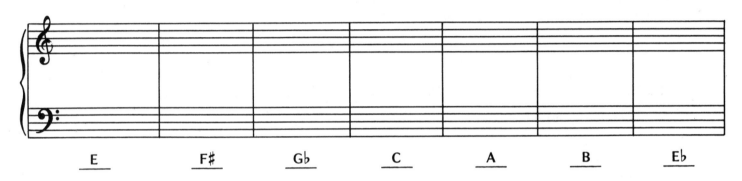

E   F#   Gb   C   A   B   Eb

Draw two space notes for each given letter name. Place one on Bass Staff and one on Treble Staff. Some will be leger space notes.

Use Half Notes.

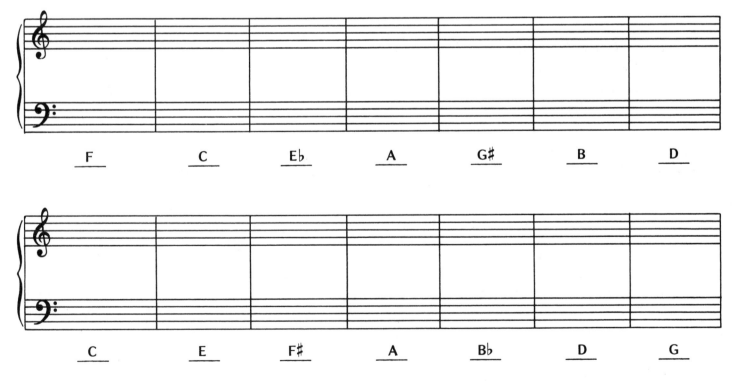

F   C   Eb   A   G#   B   D

C   E   F#   A   Bb   D   G

FDL 736

LESSON No. 26 - Drawing And Spelling Accidentals

Write letter names for the following sharps.

Ex.

C

Draw sharps on the indicated lines.

1   5   4   3   2   4   5   2

Draw sharps on the indicated spaces.

4   1   3   2   1   3   4   2

Write letter names for the following flats.

Draw flats on the indicated lines.

5   1   3   2   4   3   2   4

Draw flats on the indicated spaces.

3   1   4   2   4   2   3   1

Write letter names for the following naturals.

Draw naturals on the indicated lines.

3   1   2   4   5   1   4   3

Draw naturals on the indicated spaces.

1   4   2   3   2   1   4   3

FDL 736

LESSON No. 27 - Note Spelling In Specific Keys

Write letter names for the following notes. Be sure to observe the Key Signature.

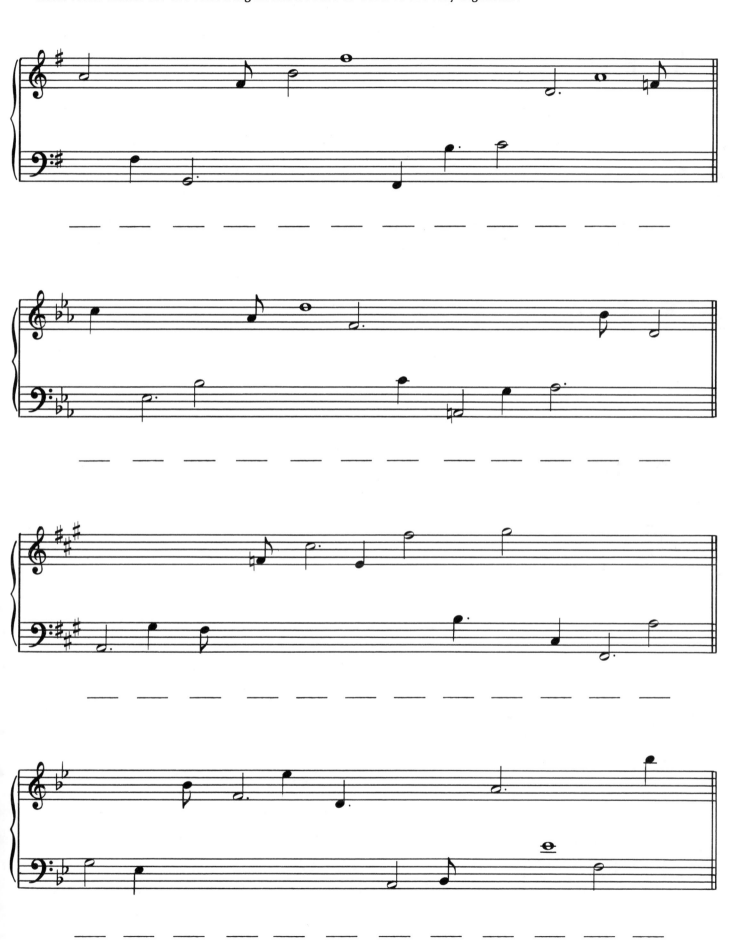

LESSON No. 28 - Note Spelling - Primary Chords

Write letter names for the notes of the following Primary Chords. Be sure to observe the Key Signatures.

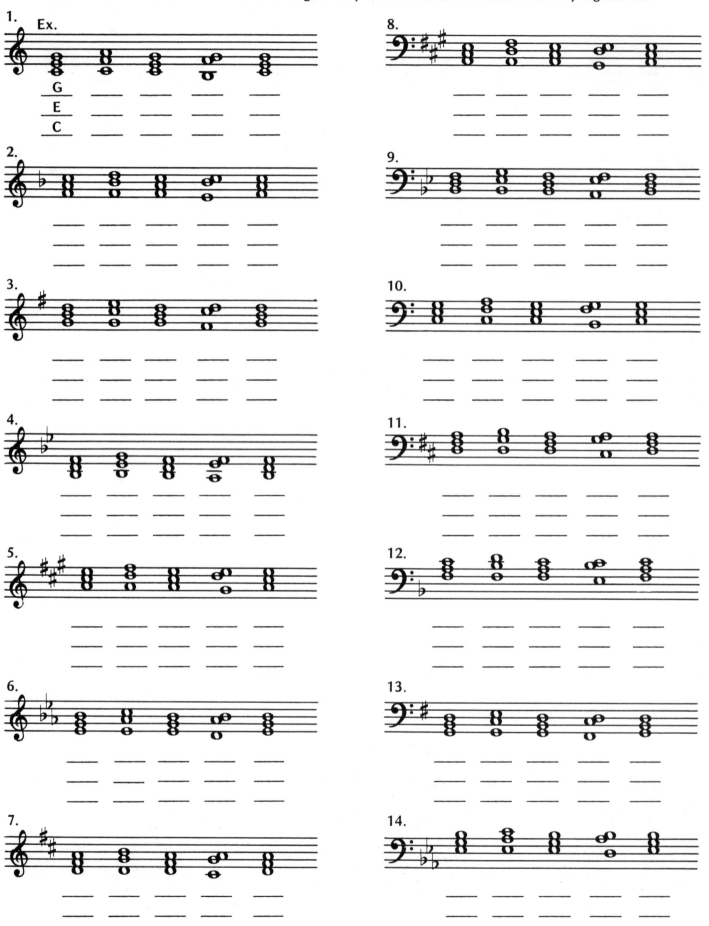

LESSON No. 29 - Note Spelling - Intervals

Write letter names for the following notes of the given Intervals.

LESSON No. 30 - Note Spelling - Grand Staff

Write letter names for the following notes. They spell words.

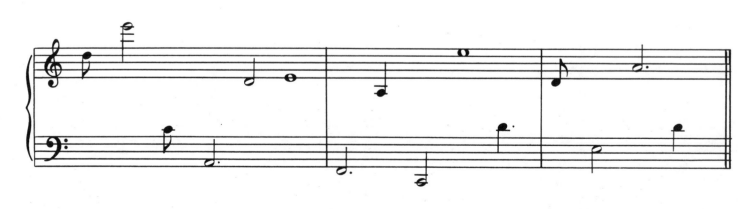